Love Is More Thicker Than Forget
and other poems

E.E. CUMMINGS

Love Is More Thicker Than Forget
and other poems

Edited by
Dr. Adyasha Das

STUDENTS UNIVERSE
2020

STUDENTS UNIVERSE
(An imprint of Black Eagle Books)

USA address:
7464 Wisdom Lane, Dublin, OH 43016

India address:
E/312, Trident Galaxy, Kalinga Nagar,
Bhubaneswar-751003, Odisha, India

E-mail: info@blackeaglebooks.org
Website: www.blackeaglebooks.org

LOVE IS MORE THICKER THAN FORGET AND OTHER POEMS
by **E.E. CUMMINGS**

Edited by **Dr. Adyasha Das**

Copyright © **Students Universe**

All rights reserved. No part of this publication may be reproduced, stored in a retrieval system, or transmitted, in any form or by any means, electronic, mechanical, photocopying, recording or otherwise without the prior permission of the publisher.

Cover & Interior Design: Ezy's Publication

ISBN- 978-1-64560-117-3 (Paperback)

Printed in United States of America

STUDENTS UNIVERSE
(An imprint of Black Eagle Books)

USA address:
7464 Wisdom Lane, Dublin, OH 43016

India address:
E/312, Trident Galaxy, Kalinga Nagar,
Bhubaneswar-751003, Odisha, India

E-mail: info@blackeaglebooks.org
Website: www.blackeaglebooks.org

LOVE IS MORE THICKER THAN FORGET AND OTHER POEMS
by E.E. CUMMINGS

Edited by **Dr. Adyasha Das**

Copyright © **Students Universe**

All rights reserved. No part of this publication may be reproduced, stored in a retrieval system, or transmitted, in any form or by any means, electronic, mechanical, photocopying, recording or otherwise without the prior permission of the publisher.

Cover & Interior Design: Ezy's Publication

ISBN- 978-1-64560-117-3 (Paperback)

Printed in United States of America

E.E. CUMMINGS

Love Is More Thicker Than Forget
and other poems

Edited by
Dr. Adyasha Das

STUDENTS UNIVERSE
2020

CONTENTS

Foreword / Dr. Adyasha Das	5
dreaming in marble all the castle lay	13
thee will i praise between those rivers whose	15
All in green went my love riding	17
cruelly, love	19
when god lets my body be	20
Thou aged unreluctant earth	21
And still the mad magnificent herald Spring	23
Lover, lead forth thy love unto that bed	25
if i believe	27
I like	29
after five	30
Humanity i love you	31
Lady of Silence	32
death in her eyes	34
as usual i did not find him in cafes	35
the dress was a suspicious madder	38
spring omnipotent goddess Thou	40
"next to of course god america i	42
The Cambridge ladies who live in furnished souls	43
Anyone Lived in a Pretty How Town	44
i carry your heart with me	46
Love Is More Thicker Than Forget	47
It Is At Moments After I Have Dreamed	48
may i feel said he	49
since feeling is first	51
pity this busy monster, manunkind	52
Puella Mea	53
why must itself up every of a park	62
The Eagle	63
from tulips and chimneys	65
lady, i will touch you with my mind	66
i like my body when it is with your	67
in a middle of a room	68
the boys i mean are not refined	69
hate blows a bubble of despair	70
Spring is like a perhaps hand	71
And What Were Roses. Perfume?For I Do	72
when my love comes to see me	73
the wind is a Lady	74
nobody loses all the time	75
Will i ever forget that precarious moment?	77
the moon looked into my window	81
touching you i say	82
if there are any heavens	83
Love Is A Place	84
Nothing False And Possible Is Love	85
Speaking Of Love	86
I Am A Beggar Always	87

You Being In Love	89
you said Is	91
the mind is its own beautiful prisoner	92
Your Little Voice...	93
this is the garden: colours come and go	94
Sometimes I Am Alive Because With	95
My Love	96
i have loved, let us see if that's all	98
Raise The Shade	99
will suddenly trees leap from winter and will	100
It May Not Always Be So	101
May My Heart Always Be Open To Little	102
because i love you	103
if i love You	104
In Time Of Daffodils	105
In The Rain	106
It Is At Moments After I Have Dreamed	107
Nothing False And Possible Is Love	108
i thank You God for most this amazing	109
Picasso	110
if i should sleep with a lady called death	111
somewhere i have never travelled, gladly beyond	112
My sweet old etcetera	113
here's to opening and upward, to leaf and to sap	115
It is funny, you will be gone some day	116
O sweet spontaneous	117
may my heart always be open to little	119
old age sticks	120
little tree	121
I Have Found What You Are Like	123
my father moved through dooms of love	124
i am a little church	127
as freedom is a breakfastfood	128
there are so many tictoc	129
if in beginning twilight of winter	130
thee will i praise between those rivers	131
When You Went Away It Was Morning	133
Let it go	134
Spring is past, and Summer's past	135
Maggie And Milly And Molly And May	137
dive for dreams	138
as we lie side by side	139
she, straddling my lap	141
A Wind Has Blown The Rain Away And Blown	142
the great advantage of being alive	143
she being Brand	144
I will wade out	146
My Love Is Building A Building	147
Yours Is The Music For No Instrument	148
Who's Most Afraid Of Death? Thou	149
Now that	150
2 little whos	151

FOREWORD

Edward Estlin "E. E. Cummings" (October 14, 1894 – September 3, 1962), popularly referred to as e e cummings, was an American poet, author, painter, essayist, and playwright. He created around 2,900 poems, two autobiographical novels, four plays, essays and several paintings. Cummings was born into a family of progressive parents who encouraged him from an early age to write poetry. He did his under-graduate and post-graduate studies at Harvard. It is at Harvard that Cummings got the opportunity to get to know many open-minded poets who subsequently influenced his writings greatly. His poems were initially published in an anthology, Eight Harvard Poets, 1917.

Immediately after his studies,

Cummings enlisted in the Norton-Harjes Ambulance Corps in France during World War I. In course of the war, he was imprisoned on the allegation of spying. He was then detained in an internment camp and this experience left a deep imprint on his mind. An avid lover of art, he studied it at Paris after his release. By this time, his literary reputation had spread far and wide. The Enormous Room (1922), Cummings first creation was a novel based on his experiences and reflections of war. Then followed his collections of poetry, Tulips and Chimneys (1923), XLI Poems (1925), and & (1925).

Cummings' poems challenged the age-old, stereo-typed conventions of the usage of language. He loved to experiment with new ideas of using words. In his writings, at times he avoided using punctuation or complete words and mostly did not use capital letters. He creatively adjusted standard syntax in his writings, with adjectives functioning as nouns.

"Cummings' experimental poetry appear to be attempts to blur boundaries and experiment with spatial poetry or temporal painting producing poems whose sounds we have to see and whose shapes we have to hear. Cummings is both a painter and a poet, and in dealing with his art, the two fields are in close relation to each other, or the two might actually be one field, as he himself wanted to be understood; "my poems are essentially pictures".   (Norman123).

The poems of Cummings convey a combined flavour of exuberance, distinctiveness and a nonconformist originality. His works are probably the most easily recognized of all American poetry. A constant quest for novel ways of expression led him to several innovative and stylistic discoveries. Cummings remains ever fresh in memory because of his conviction for the creative celebration of life and love, his reliance on the individual self and freedom of expression. The readers of Cummings' works instantly note the uncommon typographical designs as well as the fine ingenuity of his poetic vision.

In the 'nonlectures' at the Harvard University, Cummings had stated: *'So far as I am concerned, poetry and every other art was, is, and forever will be strictly and distinctly a question of individuality'.*

Poet Horace Gregory opined that in Cummings' poetry *'one is refreshed by the revival of courtly music and compliment, of poetic wit, and the art of burlesque'.*

He won the appreciation of many of his contemporaries who had attained fame. Graves, Marianne Moore, Dos Passoss, Williams, Auden, Spencer, etc have always admired him for his poetic craftsmanship.

Cummings's erotic poems and drawings have remained ageless and delight his readers. Norman Friedman had stated, "*Love was always and still is Cummings' chief subject of interest*". These poems stand out for the use of sexual metaphors. From the famed "*may I feel said he*" and "*i like my body when it is with your*" to "*she being brand*", the poems range from the delicate and subtle to being outright provocative and sexually explicit.

Cummings was popular as one of the most sensitive and profound lyric poets, unique for his originality. In his own words, Cummings writes about *'ecstasy and anguish, being and becoming; the immortality of the creative imagination and the indomitability of the human spirit'.* Throughout his life and writing career he made a focused effort to create poetry free of the trappings of linguistic antiquities. His poetry became honest reflections of his uninhibited vision of the inner and outer worlds. He was truly a poet ahead of his times. Cummings' poetry is timeless for its imaginative amalgamation of the traditional with modernism. His adroit expressions consisting of typographical twists, unconventional spacing and punctuation, peculiar use of capital and lower case letters, the splitting of the parts of a word or words and several other manoeuvres reveal his close affinity with painting.

Cummings poetry reflects the transition from eroticism to transcendence, from the world of knowledge to the realm of wisdom. This collection of one hundred selected poems of Cummings span the entire range of his creations, from the early writings to poems written much later. From being thought-provoking and humorous to sensitive and profound portrayals, these poems represent his creativity at its best.

A time for growing and a time for dying:
a night for silence and a day for singing
but more than all (all your more than e~·cs
tell me) there is a time for timelessness.
e.e cummings (95 poem.~. No. II)

Dr. Adyasha Das

life's not a paragraph And death i think is no parenthesis.

amalgamation of the traditional with modernism. His adroit expressions consisting of typographical twists, unconventional spacing and punctuation, peculiar use of capital and lower case letters, the splitting of the parts of a word or words and several other manoeuvres reveal his close affinity with painting.

Cummings poetry reflects the transition from eroticism to transcendence, from the world of knowledge to the realm of wisdom. This collection of one hundred selected poems of Cummings span the entire range of his creations, from the early writings to poems written much later. From being thought-provoking and humorous to sensitive and profound portrayals, these poems represent his creativity at its best.

A time for growing and a time for dying:
a night for silence and a day for singing
but more than all (all your more than e~·cs
tell me) there is a time for timelessness.
e.e cummings (95 poem.~. No. II)

Dr. Adyasha Das

celebration of life and love, his reliance on the individual self and freedom of expression. The readers of Cummings' works instantly note the uncommon typographical designs as well as the fine ingenuity of his poetic vision.

In the 'nonlectures' at the Harvard University, Cummings had stated: *'So far as I am concerned, poetry and every other art was, is, and forever will be strictly and distinctly a question of individuality'.*

Poet Horace Gregory opined that in Cummings' poetry *'one is refreshed by the revival of courtly music and compliment, of poetic wit, and the art of burlesque'.*

He won the appreciation of many of his contemporaries who had attained fame. Graves, Marianne Moore, Dos Passoss, Williams, Auden, Spencer, etc have always admired him for his poetic craftsmanship.

Cummings's erotic poems and drawings have remained ageless and delight his readers. Norman Friedman had stated, "*Love was always and still is Cummings' chief subject of interest*". These poems stand out for the use of sexual metaphors. From the famed "*may I feel said he*" and "*i like my body when it is with your*" to "*she being brand*", the poems range from the delicate and subtle to being outright provocative and sexually explicit.

Cummings was popular as one of the most sensitive and profound lyric poets, unique for his originality. In his own words, Cummings writes about *'ecstasy and anguish, being and becoming; the immortality of the creative imagination and the indomitability of the human spirit'.* Throughout his life and writing career he made a focused effort to create poetry free of the trappings of linguistic antiquities. His poetry became honest reflections of his uninhibited vision of the inner and outer worlds. He was truly a poet ahead of his times. Cummings' poetry is timeless for its imaginative

1.

dreaming in marble all the castle lay

dreaming in marble all the castle lay
like some gigantic ghost-flower born of night
blossoming in white towers to the moon,
soft sighed the passionate darkness to the tune
of tiny troubadours, and(phantom-white)
dumb-blooming boughs let fall their glorious snows,
and the unearthly sweetness of a rose
swam upward from the troubled heart of May;
a Winged Passion woke and one by one
there fell upon the night, like angel's tears,
the syllables of that mysterious prayer,
and as an opening lily drowsy-fair
(when from her couch of poppy petals peers
the sleepy morning)gently draws apart
her curtains, and lays bare her trembling heart,
with beads of dew made jewels by the sun,
so one high shining tower(which as a glass
turned light to flame and blazed with snowy fire)
unfolding, gave the moon a nymphlike face,
a form whose snowy symmetry of grace
haunted the limbs as music haunts the lyre,
a creature of white hands, who letting fall

a thread of lustre from the castle wall
glided, a drop of radiance, to the grass—
shunning the sudden moonbeam's treacherous snare
she sought the harbouring dark, and(catching up
her delicate silk)all white, with shining feet,
went forth into the dew: right wildly beat
her heart at every kiss of daisy-cup,
and from her cheek the beauteous colour went
with every bough that reverently bent
to touch the yellow wonder of her hair.

2.

thee will i praise between those rivers whose

(thee will i praise between those rivers whose
white voices pass upon forgetting(fail
me not)whose courseless waters are a gloat
of silver; o'er whose night three willows wail,
a slender dimness in the unshapeful hour
making dear moan in tones of stroked flower;
let not thy lust one threaded moment lose:
haste)the very shadowy sheep float
free upon terrific pastures pale,
whose tall mysterious shepherd lifts a cheek
teartroubled to the momentary wind
with guiding smile, lips wisely minced for blown
kisses, condemnatory fingers thinned
of pity—so he stands counting the moved
myriads wonderfully loved,
(hasten, it is the moment which shall seek
all blossoms that do learn, scents of not known
musics in whose careful eyes are dinned;
and the people of perfect darkness fills

his mind who will their hungering whispers hear
with weepings soundless, saying of "alas
we were chaste on earth we ghosts: hark to the sheer
cadence of our grey flesh in the gloom!
and still to be immortal is our doom;
but a rain frailly raging whom the hills
sink into and their sunsets, it shall pass.
Our feet tread sleepless meadows sweet with fear")
then be with me: unseriously seem
by the perusing greenness of thy thought
my golden soul fabulously to glue
in a superior terror; be thy taut
flesh silver, like the currency of faint
cities eternal—ere the sinless taint
of thy long sinful arms about me dream
shall my love wholly taste thee as a new
wine from steep hills by darkness softly brought—
(be with me in the sacred witchery
of almostness which May makes follow soon
on the sweet heels of passed afterday,
clothe thy soul's coming merely, with a croon
of mingling robes musically revealed
in rareness: let thy twain eyes deeply wield
a noise of petals falling silently
through the far-spaced possible nearaway
from huge trees drenched by a rounding moon)

his mind who will their hungering whispers hear
with weepings soundless, saying of "alas
we were chaste on earth we ghosts: hark to the sheer
cadence of our grey flesh in the gloom!
and still to be immortal is our doom;
but a rain frailly raging whom the hills
sink into and their sunsets, it shall pass.
Our feet tread sleepless meadows sweet with fear")
then be with me: unseriously seem
by the perusing greenness of thy thought
my golden soul fabulously to glue
in a superior terror; be thy taut
flesh silver, like the currency of faint
cities eternal—ere the sinless taint
of thy long sinful arms about me dream
shall my love wholly taste thee as a new
wine from steep hills by darkness softly brought—
(be with me in the sacred witchery
of almostness which May makes follow soon
on the sweet heels of passed afterday,
clothe thy soul's coming merely, with a croon
of mingling robes musically revealed
in rareness: let thy twain eyes deeply wield
a noise of petals falling silently
through the far-spaced possible nearaway
from huge trees drenched by a rounding moon)

2.

thee will i praise between those rivers whose

(thee will i praise between those rivers whose
white voices pass upon forgetting(fail
me not)whose courseless waters are a gloat
of silver; o'er whose night three willows wail,
a slender dimness in the unshapeful hour
making dear moan in tones of stroked flower;
let not thy lust one threaded moment lose:
haste)the very shadowy sheep float
free upon terrific pastures pale,
whose tall mysterious shepherd lifts a cheek
teartroubled to the momentary wind
with guiding smile, lips wisely minced for blown
kisses, condemnatory fingers thinned
of pity—so he stands counting the moved
myriads wonderfully loved,
(hasten, it is the moment which shall seek
all blossoms that do learn, scents of not known
musics in whose careful eyes are dinned;
and the people of perfect darkness fills

3.

All in green went my love riding

All in green went my love riding
on a great horse of
into the silver dawn.

four lean hounds crouched low and smiling
the merry deer ran before.

Fleeter be they than dappled dreams
the swift sweet deer
the red rare deer.

Four red roebuck at a white water
the cruel bugle sang before.

Horn at hip went my love riding
 riding the echo down
into the silver dawn.

four lean hounds crouched low and smiling
the level meadows ran before.

Softer be they than slippered sleep
the lean lithe deer
the fleet flown deer.

Four fleet does at a gold valley
the famished arrow sang before.

Bow at belt went my love riding
riding the mountain down
into the silver dawn.

four lean hounds crouched low and smiling
the sheer peaks ran before.

Paler be they than daunting death
the sleek slim deer
the tall tense deer.

Four tall stags at a green mountain
the lucky hunter sang before.

All in green went my love riding
on a great horse of gold
into the silver dawn.

four lean hounds crouched low and smiling
my heart fell dead before.

4.

cruelly, love

cruelly, love
walk the autumn long;
the last flower in whose hair,
thy lips are cold with songs
for which is
first to wither, to pass?
shallowness of sunlight
falls and, cruelly,
across the grass
Comes the
moon
love, walk the
autumn
love, for the last
flower in the hair withers;
thy hair is acold with
dreams,
love thou art frail
—walk the longness of autumn
smile dustily to the people,
for winter
who crookedly care

5.

when god lets my body be

when god lets my body be

From each brave eye shall sprout a tree
fruit that dangles therefrom

the purpled world will dance upon
Between my lips which did sing

a rose shall beget the spring
that maidens whom passion wastes

will lay between their little breasts
My strong fingers beneath the snow

Into strenuous birds shall go
my love walking in the grass

their wings will touch with her face
and all the while shall my heart be

With the bulge and nuzzle of the sea

6

Thou aged unreluctant earth

Thou aged unreluctant earth who dost
with quivering continual thighs invite
the thrilling rain the slender paramour
to toy with thy extraordinary lust,
(the sinuous rain which rising from thy bed
steals to his wife the sky and hour by hour
wholly renews her pale flesh with delight)
—immortally whence are the high gods fled?
Speak elm eloquent pandar with thy nod
significant to the ecstatic earth
in token of his coming whom her soul
burns to embrace—and didst thou know the god
from but the imprint of whose cloven feet
the shrieking dryad sought her leafy goal,
at the mere echo of whose shining mirth
the furious hearts of mountains ceased to beat?
Wind beautifully who wanderest
over smooth pages of forgotten joy
proving the peaceful theorems of the flowers
—didst e'er depart upon more exquisite quest?
and did thy fortunate fingers sometime dwell
(within a greener shadow of secret bowers)
among the curves of that delicious boy

whose serious grace one goddess loved too well?
Chryselephantine Zeus Olympian
sceptred colossus of the Pheidian soul
whose eagle frights creation, in whose palm
Nike presents the crown sweetest to man,
whose lilied robe the sun's white hands emboss,
betwixt whose absolute feet anoint with calm
of intent stars circling the acerb pole
poises, smiling, the diadumenos
in whose young chiseled eyes the people saw
their once again victorious Pantarkes
(whose grace the prince of artists made him bold
to imitate between the feet of awe),
thunderer whose omnipotent brow showers
its curls of unendured eternal gold
over the infinite breast in bright degrees,
whose pillow is the graces and the hours,
father of gods and men whose subtle throne
twain sphinxes bear each with a writhing youth
caught to her brazen breasts, whose foot-stool tells
how fought the looser of the warlike zone
of her that brought forth tall Hippolytus,
lord on whose pedestal the deep expels
(over Selene's car closing uncouth)
of Helios the sweet wheels tremulous—
are there no kings in Argos, that the song
is silent, of the steep unspeaking tower
within whose brightening strictness Danae
saw the night severed and the glowing throng
descend, felt on her flesh the amorous strain
of gradual hands and yielding to that fee
her eager body's unimmortal flower
knew in the darkness a more burning rain?

whose serious grace one goddess loved too well?
Chryselephantine Zeus Olympian
sceptred colossus of the Pheidian soul
whose eagle frights creation, in whose palm
Nike presents the crown sweetest to man,
whose lilied robe the sun's white hands emboss,
betwixt whose absolute feet anoint with calm
of intent stars circling the acerb pole
poises, smiling, the diadumenos
in whose young chiseled eyes the people saw
their once again victorious Pantarkes
(whose grace the prince of artists made him bold
to imitate between the feet of awe),
thunderer whose omnipotent brow showers
its curls of unendured eternal gold
over the infinite breast in bright degrees,
whose pillow is the graces and the hours,
father of gods and men whose subtle throne
twain sphinxes bear each with a writhing youth
caught to her brazen breasts, whose foot-stool tells
how fought the looser of the warlike zone
of her that brought forth tall Hippolytus,
lord on whose pedestal the deep expels
(over Selene's car closing uncouth)
of Helios the sweet wheels tremulous—
are there no kings in Argos, that the song
is silent, of the steep unspeaking tower
within whose brightening strictness Danae
saw the night severed and the glowing throng
descend, felt on her flesh the amorous strain
of gradual hands and yielding to that fee
her eager body's unimmortal flower
knew in the darkness a more burning rain?

6

Thou aged unreluctant earth

Thou aged unreluctant earth who dost
with quivering continual thighs invite
the thrilling rain the slender paramour
to toy with thy extraordinary lust,
(the sinuous rain which rising from thy bed
steals to his wife the sky and hour by hour
wholly renews her pale flesh with delight)
—immortally whence are the high gods fled?
Speak elm eloquent pandar with thy nod
significant to the ecstatic earth
in token of his coming whom her soul
burns to embrace—and didst thou know the god
from but the imprint of whose cloven feet
the shrieking dryad sought her leafy goal,
at the mere echo of whose shining mirth
the furious hearts of mountains ceased to beat?
Wind beautifully who wanderest
over smooth pages of forgotten joy
proving the peaceful theorems of the flowers
—didst e'er depart upon more exquisite quest?
and did thy fortunate fingers sometime dwell
(within a greener shadow of secret bowers)
among the curves of that delicious boy

7

And still the mad magnificent herald Spring

And still the mad magnificent herald Spring
assembles beauty from forgetfulness
with the wild trump of April: witchery
of sound and odour drives the wingless thing
man forth into bright air, for now the red
leaps in the maple's cheek, and suddenly
by shining hordes in sweet unserious dress
ascends the golden crocus from the dead.
On dappled dawn forth rides the pungent sun
with hooded day preening upon his hand
followed by gay untimid final flowers
(which dressed in various tremulous armor stun
the eyes of ragged earth who sees them pass)
while hunted from his kingdom winter cowers,
seeing green armies steadily expand
hearing the spear-song of the marching grass.

A silver sudden parody of snow
tickles the air to golden tears, and hark!
the flicker's laughing yet, while on the hills
the pines deepen to whispers primeval and throw
backward their foreheads to the barbarous bright
sky, and suddenly from the valley thrills
the unimaginable upward lark

and drowns the earth and passes into light
(slowly in life's serene perpetual round
a pale world gathers comfort to her soul,
hope richly scattered by the abundant sun
invades the new mosaic of the ground
—let but the incurious curtaining dusk be drawn
surpassing nets are sedulously spun
to snare the brutal dew,—the authentic scroll
of fairie hands and vanishing with dawn).
Spring, that omits no mention of desire
in every curved and curling thing, yet holds
continuous intercourse—through skies and trees
the lilac's smoke the poppy's pompous fire
the pansy's purple patience and the grave
frailty of daises—by what rare unease
revealed of teasingly transparent folds—
with man's poor soul superlatively brave.
Surely from robes of particoloured peace
with mouth flower-faint and undiscovered eyes
and dim slow perfect body amorous
(whiter than lilies which are born and cease
for being whiter than this world)exhales
the hovering high perfume curious
of that one month for whom the whole year dies,
risen at length from palpitating veils.
O still miraculous May! O shining girl
of time untarnished ! 0 small intimate
gently primeval hands, frivolous feet
divine.'O singular and breathless pearl!
O indefinable frail ultimate pose!
0 visible beatitude sweet sweet
intolerable.'silence immaculate
of god's evasive audible great rose!

8

Lover, lead forth thy love unto that bed

Lover, lead forth thy love unto that bed
prepared by whitest hands of waiting years,
curtained with wordless worship absolute,
unto the certain altar at whose head
stands that clear candle whose expecting breath
exults upon the tongue of flame half-mute,
(haste ere some thrush with silver several tears
complete the perfumed paraphrase of death).
Now is the time when all occasional things
close into silence, only one tree, one
svelte translation of eternity
unto the pale meaning of heaven clings,
(whose million leaves in winsome indolence
simmer upon thinking twilight momently)
as down the oblivious west's numerous dun
magnificence conquers magnificence.
In heaven's intolerable athanor
inimitably tortured the base day
utters at length her soft intrinsic hour,
and from those tenuous fires which more and more
sink and are lost the divine alchemist,
the magus of creation, lifts a flower—
whence is the world's insufferable clay
clothed with incognizable amethyst.
Lady at whose imperishable smile

the amazed doves flicker upon sunny wings
as if in terror of eternity,
(or seeming that they would mistrust a while
the moving of beauteous dead mouths throughout
that very proud transparent company
of quivering ghosts-of-love which scarcely sings
drifting in slow diaphanous faint rout),
queen in the inconceivable embrace
of whose tremendous hair that blossom stands
whereof is most desire, yet less than those
twain perfect roses whose ambrosial grace,
goddess, thy crippled thunder-forging groom
or the loud lord of skipping maenads knows,—
having Discordia's apple in thy hands,
which the scared shepherd gave thee for his doom—

 thou within the chancel of whose charms
the tall boy god of everlasting war
received the shuddering sacrament of sleep,
betwixt whose cool incorrigible arms
impaled upon delicious mystery,
with gaunt limbs reeking of the whispered deep,
deliberate groping ocean fondled o'er
the warm long flower of unchastity,
imperial Cytherea, from frail foam
sprung with irrevocable nakedness
to strike the young world into smoking song—
as the first star perfects the sensual dome
of darkness, and the sweet strong final bird
transcends the sight,O thou to whom belong
the hearts of lovers!—I beseech thee bless
thy suppliant singer and his wandering word.

9

if i believe

if i believe
in death be sure
of this
it is
because you have loved me,
moon and sunset
stars and flowers
gold crescendo and silver muting
of seatides
i trusted not,
one night
when in my fingers
drooped your shining body
when my heart
sang between your perfect
breasts
darkness and beauty of stars
was on my mouth petals danced
against my eyes
and down
the singing reaches of
my soul

spoke
the greengreeting
paledeparting
irrevocable
sea
i knew thee death.
and when
i have offered up each fragrant
night, when all my days
shall have before a certain
face become
white
perfume
only,
from the ashes
then
thou wilt rise and thou
wilt come to her and brush
the mischief from her eyes and fold
her
mouth the new
flower with
thy unimaginable
wings, where dwells the breath
of all persisting stars

10

I like

I like
to think that on
the flower you gave me when we
loved
the fardeparted
mouth sweetly-saluted
lingers.
if one marvel
seeing the hunger of my
lips for a dead thing,
i shall instruct
him silently with becoming
steps to seek
your face and i
entreat, by certain foolish perfect
hours
dead too,
if that he come receive
him as your lover sumptuously
being
kind
because i trust him to
your grace, and for
in his own land
he is called death.

11

after five

after five
times the poem
of thy remembrance
surprises with refrain
of unreasoning summer
that by responding
ways cloaked with renewal
my body turns toward
thee
again for the stars have been
finished in the nobler trees and
the language of leaves repeats
eventual perfection
while east deserves of dawn,
i lie at length, breathing
with shut eyes
the sweet earth where thou liest

11

after five

after five
times the poem
of thy remembrance
surprises with refrain
of unreasoning summer
that by responding
ways cloaked with renewal
my body turns toward
thee
again for the stars have been
finished in the nobler trees and
the language of leaves repeats
eventual perfection
while east deserves of dawn,
i lie at length, breathing
with shut eyes
the sweet earth where thou liest

10

I like

I like
to think that on
the flower you gave me when we
loved
the fardeparted
mouth sweetly-saluted
lingers.
if one marvel
seeing the hunger of my
lips for a dead thing,
i shall instruct
him silently with becoming
steps to seek
your face and i
entreat, by certain foolish perfect
hours
dead too,
if that he come receive
him as your lover sumptuously
being
kind
because i trust him to
your grace, and for
in his own land
he is called death.

12

Humanity i love you

Humanity i love you
because you would rather black the boots of
success than enquire whose soul dangles from his
watch-chain which would be embarrassing for both
parties and because you
unflinchingly applaud all
songs containing the words country home and
mother when sung at the old howard
Humanity i love you because
when you're hard up you pawn your
intelligence to buy a drink and when
you're flush pride keeps
you from the pawn shop and
because you are continually committing
nuisances but more
especially in your own house
Humanity i love you because you
are perpetually putting the secret of
life in your pants and forgetting
it's there and sitting down
on it
and because you are
forever making poems in the lap
of death Humanity
i hate you

13

Lady of Silence

Lady of Silence
from the winsome cage of
thy body
rose
through the sensible
night
a
quick bird
(tenderly upon
the dark's prodigious face
thy
voice
scattering perfume-gifted
wings
suddenly escorts
with feet
sun-sheer
the smarting beauty of dawn)
the sky a silver

dissonance by the correct
fingers of April
resolved
into a
clutter of trite jewels
now like a moth with stumbling
wings flutters and flops along the
grass collides with trees and
houses and finally,
butts into the river

14

death in her eyes

death in her eyes
and it is dawn
the world
goes forth to murder dreams....
i see in the street where strong
men are digging bread
and i see the brutal faces of
people contented hideous hopeless cruel happy
and it is day,
in the mirror
i see a frail
man
dreaming
dreams
dreams in the mirror
and it
is dusk on earth
a candle is lighted
and it is dark.
the people are in their houses
the frail man is in his bed
the city
sleeps with death upon her mouth having a song in her eyes
the hours descend,
putting on stars....
in the street of the sky night walks scattering poems

15

as usual i did not find him in cafes

as usual i did not find him in cafes, the more dissolute atmosphere
of a street superimposing a numbing imperfectness upon
such peregrinations
as twilight spontaneously by inevitable tiredness of flanging
shop-girls impersonally affords furnished a soft first clue to
his innumerable whereabouts violet logic of annihilation
demonstrating
from woolworthian pinnacle a capable millennium of faces
meshing with my curiously instant appreciation
exposed his hibernative
contours,

aimiable immensity impeccably extending the courtesy
of five o'clock
became the omen of his presence it was spring by the
way in the
soiled canary-cage of largest existence
(when he would extemporise the innovation of muscular-
ity upon the
most crimson assistance of my comforter a click of
deciding glory

inflicted to the negative silence that primeval exposure
whose electric
solidity remembers some accurately profuse scratchings in a
recently discovered cave, the carouse of geometrical
putrescence
whereto my invariably commendable room has been
forever subject his
Earliest word wheeled out on the sunny dump of
oblivion)

a tiny dust finely arising at the integration of my soul i
coughed
,naturally

the skinny voice
of the leather-faced
woman with the crimson
nose and coquettishly cocked
bonnet
having ceased the
captain
announces that as three
dimes seven nickels and ten
pennies have been deposited upon
the drum there is need
of just twenty five cents
dear friends
to make it an even
dollar whereupon
the Divine Average who was
attracted by the inspired
sister's howling moves

off
will anyone tell him why he should

blow two bits for the coming of Christ Jesus

?
??
???
!

nix, kid

16

the dress was a suspicious madder

the dress was a suspicious madder, importing the cruelty
of roses.
The exciting simplicity of her hipless body, pausing to
invent imperceptible
bulgings of the pretended breasts, forked in surprisable
unliving eyes chopped by a swollen inanity of picture hat.

the arms hung ugly., the hands sharp and impertinently dead.
expression began with the early cessation of her skirt,
fleshless
melody of the, keenly lascivious legs, painful ankles large
acute brutal feet propped on irrelevantly ferocious heels.

Her gasping slippery body moved with the hideous
spontaneity
of a solemn mechanism, beneath her drab tempo of
hasteful futility
lived brilliantly the enormous rhythm of absurdity.

skin like the poisonous fragility of ice newly formed
upon an old
pool. Her nose was small, exact, stupid. mouth normal,

large, unclever.
hair genuinely artificial, unpleasantly tremendous.

under flat lusts of light her nice concupiscence appeared rounded.

if she were alive, death was amusing

17

spring omnipotent goddess Thou

SPRING omnipotent goddess Thou
dost stuff parks
with overgrown pimply
chevaliers and gumchewing giggly

damosels Thou dost
persuade to serenade
his lady the musical tom-cat
Thou dost inveigle

into crossing sidewalks the
unwary june-bug and the frivolous
angleworm
Thou dost hang canary birds in parlour windows

Spring slattern of seasons
you have soggy legs
and a muddy petticoat
drowsy

is your hair your
eyes are sticky with
dream and you have a sloppy body from

being brought to bed of crocuses
when you sing in your whisky voice
the grass rises on the head of the earth
and all the trees are put on edge

spring
of the excellent jostle of
thy hips
and the superior

slobber of your breasts i
am so very fond that my
soul inside of me hollers
for thou comest

and your hands are the snow and thy
fingers are the rain
and your
feet O your feet

freakish
feet feet incorrigible

ragging the world

18

next to of course god america i

"next to of course god america i
love you land of the pilgrims' and so forth oh
say can you see by the dawn's early my
country tis of centuries come and go
and are no more what of it we should worry
in every language even deafanddumb
thy sons acclaim your glorious name by gorry
by jingo by gee by gosh by gum
why talk of beauty what could be more beaut-
iful than these heroic happy dead
who rushed like lions to the roaring slaughter
they did not stop to think they died instead
then shall the voice of liberty be mute?"
He spoke. And drank rapidly a glass of water

18

next to of course god america i

"next to of course god america i
love you land of the pilgrims' and so forth oh
say can you see by the dawn's early my
country tis of centuries come and go
and are no more what of it we should worry
in every language even deafanddumb
thy sons acclaim your glorious name by gorry
by jingo by gee by gosh by gum
why talk of beauty what could be more beaut-
iful than these heroic happy dead
who rushed like lions to the roaring slaughter
they did not stop to think they died instead
then shall the voice of liberty be mute?"
He spoke. And drank rapidly a glass of water

being brought to bed of crocuses
when you sing in your whisky voice
the grass rises on the head of the earth
and all the trees are put on edge

spring
of the excellent jostle of
thy hips
and the superior

slobber of your breasts i
am so very fond that my
soul inside of me hollers
for thou comest

and your hands are the snow and thy
fingers are the rain
and your
feet O your feet

freakish
feet feet incorrigible

ragging the world

19

The Cambridge ladies who
live in furnished souls

the Cambridge ladies who live in furnished souls
are unbeautiful and have comfortable minds
(also, with the church's protestant blessings
daughters, unscented shapeless spirited)
they believe in Christ and Longfellow, both dead,
are invariably interested in so many things-
at the present writing one still finds
delighted fingers knitting for the is it Poles?
perhaps.   While permanent faces coyly bandy
scandal of Mrs. N and Professor D
....the Cambridge ladies do not care, above
Cambridge if sometimes in its box of
sky lavender and cornerless, the
moon rattles like a fragment of angry candy

20

Anyone Lived in a Pretty How Town

anyone lived in a pretty how town
(with up so floating many bells down)
spring summer autumn winter
he sang his didn't he danced his did.

Women and men(both little and small)
cared for anyone not at all
they sowed their isn't they reaped their same
sun moon stars rain

children guessed(but only a few
and down they forgot as up they grew
autumn winter spring summer)
that no-one loved him more by more

when by now and tree by leaf
she laughed his joy she cried his grief
bird by snow and stir by still
anyone's any was all to her

someones married their everyones
laughed their cryings and did their dance

(sleep wake hope and then)they
said their nevers they slept their dream

stars rain sun moon
(and only the snow can begin to explain
how children are apt to forget to remember
with up so floating many bells down)

one day anyone died i guess
(and noone stooped to kiss his face)
busy folk buried them side by side
little by little and was by was

all by all and deep by deep
and more by more they dream their sleep
no one and anyone earth by april
wish by spirit and if by yes.

Women and men (both dong and ding)
summer autumn winter spring
reaped their sowing and went their came
sun moon stars rain

21

i carry your heart with me

i carry your heart with me(i carry it in
my heart)i am never without it(anywhere
i go you go, my dear; and whatever is done
by only me is your doing, my darling)
                              i fear
no fate(for you are my fate, my sweet)i want
no world(for beautiful you are my world, my true)
and it's you are whatever a moon has always meant
and whatever a sun will always sing is you

here is the deepest secret nobody knows
(here is the root of the root and the bud of the bud
and the sky of the sky of a tree called life;which grows
higher than soul can hope or mind can hide)
and this is the wonder that's keeping the stars apart

i carry your heart(i carry it in my heart)

22

Love Is More Thicker Than Forget

Love is more thicker than forget
more thinner than recall
more seldom than a wave is wet
more frequent than to fail
It's most mad and moonly
and less it shall unbe
than all the sea which only
is deeper than the seaLove is more always than to win
less never than alive
less bigger than the least begin
less litter than forgive It's most sane and sunly
and more it cannot die
than all the sky which only
is higher than the sky

23

It Is At Moments After I Have Dreamed

It is at moments after i have dreamed
of the rare entertainment of your eyes,
when(being fool to fancy)i have deemed
with your peculiar mouth my heart made wise;
at moments when the glassy darkness holds
the genuine apparition of your smile
(it was through tears always)and silence moulds
such strangeness as was mine a little while;
moments when my once more illustrious arms
are filled with fascination, when my breast
wears the intolerant brightness of your charms:
one pierced moment whiter than the rest– turning from
the tremendous lie of sleep
i watch the roses of the day grow deep

24

may i feel said he

may i feel said he
(i'll squeal said she
just once said he)
it's fun said she

(may i touch said he
how much said she
a lot said he)
why not said she

(let's go said he
not too far said she
what's too far said he
where you are said she)

may i stay said he
which way said she
like this said he
if you kiss said she

may i move said he
is it love said she)
if you're willing said he
(but you're killing said she

but it's life said he
but your wife said she
now said he)
ow said she

(tiptop said he
don't stop said she
oh no said he)
go slow said she
(cccome?said he
ummm said she)
you're divine!said he
(you are Mine said she)

25

since feeling is first

since feeling is first
who pays any attention
to the syntax of things
will never wholly kiss you;

wholly to be a fool
while Spring is in the world

my blood approves,
and kisses are a better fate
than wisdom
lady i swear by all flowers. Don't cry
– the best gesture of my brain is less than
your eyelids' flutter which says

we are for each other; then
laugh, leaning back in my arms
for life's not a paragraph

And death i think is no parenthesis

26

pity this busy monster, manunkind

pity this busy monster, manunkind,

not. Progress is a comfortable disease:
your victim (death and life safely beyond)

plays with the bigness of his littleness
— electrons deify one razorblade
into a mountainrange; lenses extend
unwish through curving wherewhen till unwish
returns on its unself.
                        A world of made
is not a world of born — pity poor flesh

and trees, poor stars and stones, but never this
fine specimen of hypermagical

ultraomnipotence. We doctors know

a hopeless case if — listen: there's a hell
of a good universe next door; let's go

27

Puella Mea

Harun Omar and Master Hafiz
keep your dead beautiful ladies.
Mine is a little lovelier
than any of your ladies were.

In her perfectest array
my lady, moving in the day,
is a little stranger thing
than crisp Sheba with her king
in the morning wandering.
Through the young and awkward hours
my lady perfectly moving,
through the new world scarce astir
my fragile lady wandering
in whose perishable poise
is the mystery of Spring
(with her beauty more than snow
dexterous and fugitive
my very frail lady drifting
distinctly, moving like a myth
in the uncertain morning, with
April feet like sudden flowers

and all her body filled with May)
— moving in the unskilful day
my lady utterly alive,
to me is a more curious thing
(a thing more nimble and complete)
than ever to Judea's king
were the shapely sharp cunning
and withal delirious feet
of the Princess Salomé
carefully dancing in the noise
of Herod's silence, long ago.

If she a little turn her head
I know that I am wholly dead:
nor ever did on such a throat
the lips of Tristram slowly dote,
La beale Isoud whose leman was.
And if my lady look at me
(with her eyes which like two elves
incredibly amuse themselves)
with a look of faerie,
perhaps a little suddenly
(as sometimes the improbable
beauty of my lady will)
— at her glance my spirit shies
rearing (as in the miracle
of a lady who had eyes
which the king's horses might not kill.)
    But should my lady smile, it were
a flower of so pure surprise
(it were so very new a flower,
a flower so frail, a flower so glad)
as trembling used to yield with dew

when the world was young and new
(a flower such as the world had
in springtime when the world was mad
and Launcelot spoke to Guenever,
a flower which most heavy hung
with silence when the world was young
and Diarmid looked in Grania's eyes.)
   But should my lady's beauty play
at not speaking (sometimes as
it will) the silence of her face
doth immediately make
in my heart so great a noise,
as in the sharp and thirsty blood
of Paris would not all the Troys
of Helen's beauty: never did
Lord Jason (in impossible things
victorious impossibly)
so wholly burn, to undertake

Medea's rescuing eyes; nor he
when swooned the white egyptian day
who with Egypt's body lay.

Lovely as those ladies were
mine is a little lovelier.

And if she speak in her frail way,
it is wholly to bewitch
my smallest thought with a most swift
radiance wherein slowly drift
murmurous things divinely bright;
it is foolingly to smite
my spirit with the lithe free twitch

of scintillant space, with the cool writhe
of gloom truly which syncopate
some sunbeam's skilful fingerings;
it is utterly to lull
with foliate inscrutable
sweetness my soul obedient;
it is to stroke my being with
numbing forests, frolicsome,
fleetly mystical, aroam
with keen creatures of idiom
(beings alert and innocent
very deftly upon which
indolent miracles impinge)
— it is distinctly to confute
my reason with the deep caress
of every most shy thing and mute,
it is to quell me with the twinge
of all living intense things.
    Never my soul so fortunate
is (past the luck of all dead men
and loving) as invisibly when
upon her palpable solitude
a furtive occult fragrance steals,
a gesture of immaculate
perfume — whereby (with fear aglow)

my soul is wont wholly to know
the poignant instantaneous fern
whose scrupulous enchanted fronds
toward all things intrinsic yearn,
the immanent subliminal
fern of her delicious voice
(of her voice which always dwells

beside the vivid magical
impetuous and utter ponds
of dream; and very secret food
its leaves inimitable find
beyond the white authentic springs,
beyond the sweet instinctive wells,
which make to flourish the minute
spontaneous meadow of her mind)
— the vocal fern, alway which feels
the keen ecstatic actual tread
(and thereto perfectly responds)
of all things exquisite and dead,
all living things and beautiful.

(Caliph and king their ladies had
to love them and to make them glad,
when the world was young and mad,
in the city of Bagdad —
mine is a little lovelier
than any of their ladies were.)

Her body is most beauteous,
being for all things amorous
fashioned very curiously
of roses and of ivory.
The immaculate crisp head
is such as only certain dead
and careful painters love to use
for their youngest angels (whose
praising bodies in a row
between slow glories fleetly go.)
Upon a keen and lovely throat

the strangeness of her face doth float,
which in eyes and lips consists
— alway upon the mouth there trysts
curvingly a fragile smile
which like a flower lieth (while
within the eyes is dimly heard
a wistful and precarious bird.)
Springing from fragrant shoulders small,
ardent, and perfectly withal
smooth to stroke and sweet to see
as a supple and young tree,
her slim lascivious arms alight
in skilful wrists which hint at flight
— my lady's very singular
and slenderest hands moreover are
(which as lilies smile and quail)
of all things perfect the most frail.

(Whoso rideth in the tale
of Chaucer knoweth many a pair
of companions blithe and fair;
who to walk with Master Gower
in Confessio doth prefer
shall not lack for beauty there,
nor he that will amaying go
with my lord Boccaccio —
whoso knocketh at the door
of Marie and of Maleore
findeth of ladies goodly store
whose beauty did in nothing err.
If to me there shall appear
than a rose more sweetly known,
more silently than a flower,

my lady naked in her hair —
I for those ladies nothing care
nor any lady dead and gone.)

When the world was like a song
heard behind a golden door,

poet and sage and caliph had
to love them and to make them glad
ladies with lithe eyes and long
(when the world was like a flower
Omar Hafiz and Harun
loved their ladies in the moon)
— fashioned very curiously
of roses and ivory
if naked she appear to me
my flesh is an enchanted tree;
with her lips' most frail parting
my body hears the cry of Spring,
and with their frailest syllable
its leaves go crisp with miracle.

Love! — maker of my lady,
in that alway beyond this
poem or any poem she
of whose body words are afraid
perfectly beautiful is,
forgive these words which I have made.
And never boast your dead beauties,
you greatest lovers in the world!
never boast your beauties dead
who with Grania strangely fled,
who with Egypt went to bed,

whom white-thighed Semiramis
put up her mouth to wholly kiss —
never boast your dead beauties,
mine being unto me sweeter
(of whose why delicious glance
things which never more shall be,
perfect things of faerie,
are intense inhabitants;
in whose warm superlative
body do distinctly live
all sweet cities passed away —
in her flesh at break of day
are the smells of Nineveh,

in her eyes when day is gone
are the cries of Babylon.)
Diarmid Paris and Solomon,
Omar Harun and Master Hafiz,
to me your ladies are all one —
keep your dead beautiful ladies.

Eater of all things lovely — Time!
upon whose watering lips the world
poises a moment (futile, proud,
a costly morsel of sweet tears)
gesticulates, and disappears —
of all dainties which do crowd
gaily upon oblivion
sweeter than any there is one;
to touch it is the fear of rhyme —
in life's very fragile hour
(when the world was like a tale
made of laughter and of dew,

was a flight, a flower, a flame,
was a tendril fleetly curled
upon frailness) used to stroll
(very slowly) one or two
ladies like flowers made,
softly used to wholly move
slender ladies made of dream
(in the lazy world and new
sweetly used to laugh and love
ladies with crisp eyes and frail,
in the city of Bagdad.)

Keep your dead beautiful ladies
Harun Omar and Master Hafiz.

28

why must itself up every of a park

why must itself up every of a park
anus stick some quote statue unquote to
prove that a hero equals any jerk
who was afraid to dare to answer "no"?
quote citizens unquote might otherwise
forget(to err is human; to forgive
divine)that if the quote state unquote says
"kill" killing is an act of christian love.
"Nothing" in 1944 AD
"can stand against the argument of mil
itary necessity"(generalissimo e)
and echo answers "there is no appeal
from reason"(freud)—you pays your money and
you doesn't take your choice. Ain't freedom grand

29

The Eagle

It was one of those clear, sharp, mustless days
    That summer and man delight in.
Never had Heaven seemed quite so high,
Never had earth seemed quite so green,
Never had the world seemed quite so clean
Or sky so nigh.
    And I heard the Deity's voice in
        The sun's warm rays,
    And the white cloud's intricate maze,
And the blue sky's beautiful sheen.

I looked to the heavens and saw him there,—
    A black speck downward drifting,
Nearer and nearer he steadily sailed,
Nearer and nearer he slid through space,
In an unending aerial race,
    This sailor who hailed
      From the Clime of the Clouds.—Ever shifting,
        On billows of air
      And the blue sky seemed never so fair,
And the rest of the world kept pace.

On the white of his head the sun flashed bright;
    And he battled the wind with wide pinions,
Clearer and clearer the gale whistled loud,
Clearer and clearer he came into view,—
Bigger and blacker against the blue.
    Then a dragon of cloud
      Gathering all its minions
        Rushed to the fight,
    And swallowed him up in a bite;
And the sky lay empty clear through.

Long I watched. And at last afar
    Caught sight of a speck in the vastness;
Ever smaller, ever decreasing,
Ever drifting, drifting awayInto the endless realms of day;
    Finally ceasing.
    So into Heaven's vast fastness
      Vanished that bar
Of black, as a fluttering star
Goes out while still on its way.

So I lost him. But I shall always see
    In my mind
The warm, yellow sun, and the ether free;
The vista's sky, and the white cloud trailing,
    Trailing behind,—
And below the young earth's summer-green arbors,
And on high the eagle,—sailing,sailing
    Into far skies and unknown harbors

30

the bigness of cannon

the bigness of cannon
is skilful,

bit i have seen
death's clever enormous voice
which hides in a fragility
of poppies.....

i say that sometimes
on these long talkative animals
are laid fists of huger silence

i have seen all the silence
filled with vivid noiseless boys

at Roupy
i have seen
between barrages,

the night utter ripe unspeaking girls.

31

lady, i will touch you with my mind

lady, i will touch you with my mind.
touch you and touch and touch
until you give
me suddenly a smile, shyly obscene

(lady i will
touch you with my mind.) Touch
you, that is all,

lightly and you utterly will become
with infinite care

the poem which i do not write.

31

lady, i will touch you with my mind

lady, i will touch you with my mind.
touch you and touch and touch
until you give
me suddenly a smile, shyly obscene

(lady i will
touch you with my mind.) Touch
you, that is all,

lightly and you utterly will become
with infinite care

the poem which i do not write.

30

the bigness of cannon

the bigness of cannon
is skilful,

bit i have seen
death's clever enormous voice
which hides in a fragility
of poppies…..

i say that sometimes
on these long talkative animals
are laid fists of huger silence

i have seen all the silence
filled with vivid noiseless boys

at Roupy
i have seen
between barrages,

the night utter ripe unspeaking girls.

32

i like my body when it is with your

i like my body when it is with your
body. It is so quite new a thing.
Muscles better and nerves more.
i like your body. i like what it does,
i like its hows. i like to feel the spine
of your body and its bones, and the trembling
-firm-smooth ness and which i will
again and again and again
kiss, i like kissing this and that of you,
i like, slowly stroking the, shocking fuzz
of your electric fur, and what-is-it comes
over parting flesh… And eyes big love-crumbs,

and possibly i like the thrill

of under me you so quite new

33

in a middle of a room

in a middle of a room
stands a suicide
sniffing a Paper rose
smiling to a self

"somewhere it is Spring and sometimes
people are in real: imagine
somewhere real flowers, but
I can't imagine real flowers for if I

could, they would somehow
not Be real"
(so he smiles
smiling)"but I will not

everywhere be real to
you in a moment"
The is blond
with small hands

"& everything is easier
than I had guessed everything would
be; even remembering the way who
looked at whom first, anyhow dancing"

(a moon swims out of a cloud
a clock strikes midnight
a finger pulls a trigger
a bird flies into a mirror)

34

the boys i mean are not refined

the boys i mean are not refined
they go with girls who buck and bite
they do not give a fuck for luck
they hump them thirteen times a night

one hangs a hat upon her tit
one carves a cross on her behind
they do not give a shit for wit
the boys i mean are not refined

they come with girls who bite and buck
who cannot read and cannot write
who laugh like they would fall apart
and masturbate with dynamite

the boys i mean are not refined
they cannot chat of that and this
they do not give a fart for art
they kill like you would take a piss

they speak whatever's on their mind
they do whatever's in their pants
the boys i mean are not refined
they shake the mountains when they dance

35

hate blows a bubble of despair into

hate blows a bubble of despair into
hugeness world system universe and bang
-fear buries a tomorrow under woe
and up comes yesterday most green and young

pleasure and pain are merely surfaces
(one itself showing, itself hiding one)
life's only and true value neither is
love makes the little thickness of the coin

comes here a man would have from madame death
nevertheless now and without winter spring?
she'll spin that spirit her own fingers with
and give him nothing (if he should not sing)

how much more than enough for both of us
darling. And if i sing you are my voice,

36

Spring is like a perhaps hand

Spring is like a perhaps hand
(which comes carefully
out of Nowhere)arranging
a window, into which people look(while
people stare
arranging and changing placing
carefully there a strange
thing and a known thing here)and

changing everything carefully

spring is like a perhaps
Hand in a window
(carefully to
and fro moving New and
Old things, while
people stare carefully
moving a perhaps
fraction of flower here placing
an inch of air there)and

without breaking anything.

And What Were Roses. Perfume?For I Do

and what were roses. Perfume?for i do
forget...or mere Music mounting unsurely

twilight
          but here were something more maturely
childish,more beautiful almost than you.

Yet if not flower,tell me softly who

be these haunters of dreams always demurely
halfsmiling from cool faces,moving purely
with muted steps,yet somewhat proudly too—

are they not ladies,ladies of my dreams
justly touching roses their fingers whitely
live by?
         or better,
                    queens,queens laughing lightly
crowned with far colors,

                    thinking very much
of nothing and whom dawn loves most to touch

wishing by willows,bending upon streams?

38

when my love comes to see me it's

when my love comes to see me it's
just a little like music, a
little more like curving colour(say
orange)

against silence, or darkness....

the coming of my love emits
a wonderful smell in my mind,

you should see when i turn to find
her how my least heart-beat becomes less.
And then all her beauty is a vise

whose stilling lips murder suddenly me,

but of my corpse the tool her smile makes something
suddenly luminous and precise

—and then we are I and She....

what is that the hurdy-gurdy's playing

39

the wind is a Lady

the wind is a Lady with
bright slender eyes(who
moves)at sunset
and who—touches—the
hills without any reason

(i have spoken with this
indubitable and green person "Are
You the wind?" "Yes" "why do you touch flowers
as if they were unalive, as
if They were ideas?" "because, sir

things which in my mind blossom will
stumble beneath a clumsiest disguise, appear
capable of fragility and indecision

—do not suppose these
without any reason and otherwise
roses and mountains
different from the i am who wanders
imminently across the renewed world"

to me said the)wind being A lady in a **green**
dress, who; touches: the fields
(at sunset)

40

nobody loses all the time

nobody loses all the time
i had an uncle named
Sol who was a born failure and
nearly everybody said he should have gone
into vaudeville perhaps because my Uncle Sol could
sing McCann He Was A Diver on Xmas Eve like Hell Itself
which
may or may not account for the fact that my Uncle

Sol indulged in that possibly most inexcusable
of all to use a highfalootin phrase

luxuries that is or to
wit farming and be
it needlessly
added

my Uncle Sol's farm
failed because the chickens
ate the vegetables so
my Uncle Sol had a
chicken farm till the
skunks ate the chickens when

my Uncle Sol
had a skunk farm but
the skunks caught cold and
died and so
my Uncle Sol imitated the
skunks in a subtle manner

or by drowning himself in the watertank
but somebody who'd given my Uncle Sol a Victor
Victrola and records while he lived presented to
him upon the auspicious occasion of his decease a
scrumptious not to mention splendiferous funeral with
tall boys in black gloves and flowers and everything and

r remember we all cried like the Missouri
when my Uncle Sol's coffin lurched because
somebody pressed a btitton
(and down went
my Uncle
Sol

and started a worm farm)

my Uncle Sol
had a skunk farm but
the skunks caught cold and
died and so
my Uncle Sol imitated the
skunks in a subtle manner

or by drowning himself in the watertank
but somebody who'd given my Uncle Sol a Victor
Victrola and records while he lived presented to
him upon the auspicious occasion of his decease a
scrumptious not to mention splendiferous funeral with
tall boys in black gloves and flowers and everything and

r remember we all cried like the Missouri
when my Uncle Sol's coffin lurched because
somebody pressed a btitton
(and down went
my Uncle
Sol

and started a worm farm)

40

nobody loses all the time

nobody loses all the time
i had an uncle named
Sol who was a born failure and
nearly everybody said he should have gone
into vaudeville perhaps because my Uncle Sol could
sing McCann He Was A Diver on Xmas Eve like Hell Itself which
may or may not account for the fact that my Uncle

Sol indulged in that possibly most inexcusable
of all to use a highfalootin phrase

luxuries that is or to
wit farming and be
it needlessly
added

my Uncle Sol's farm
failed because the chickens
ate the vegetables so
my Uncle Sol had a
chicken farm till the
skunks ate the chickens when

41

Will i ever forget that precarious moment?

Will i ever forget that precarious moment?

As i was standing on the third rail waiting for the next train to grind me
into lifeless atoms various absurd thoughts slyly crept into my highly sexed
mind.

It seemed to me that i had first of all really made quite a mistake in being
at all born, seeing that i was wifeless and only half awake, cursed with pimples,
correctly dressed, cleanshaven above the nombril, and much to my astonishment much impressed by having once noticed(as an infantile phenomenon)George Washington almost incompletely surrounded by well-drawn icecakes beheld being too strong, in brief :an Americanos you understand that i mean what i say i believe my most intimate friends would never have gathered.

A collarbutton which had always not nothurt me not
much and in the same place.

Why according to tomorrow's paper the proletariat will
not rise yesterday.

Inexpressible itchings to be photographed with Lord
Rothermere playing with
Lord Rothermere billiards very well by moonlight with
Lord Rothermere.

A crocodile eats a native, who in revenge beats it insen-
sible with a banana,
establishing meanwhile a religious cult based on consub-
stantial intangibility.

Personne ne m'aime et j'ai les mains froides.

His Royal Highness said "peek-a-boo" and thirty tame
fleas left the prettily
embroidered howdah immediately.

Thumbprints of an angel named Frederick found on a
lightning-rod, Boston, Mass.

such were the not unhurried reflections to which my
organ of imperception gave
birth to which i should ordinarily have objected to
which, considering the background is hardly surprising if
anyone hardly should call exactly extraordinary.
We refer, of course, to my position. A bachelor incapable
of occupation, he
had long suppressed the desire to suppress the sup-

pressed desire of shall we
say: Idleness, while meaning its opposite? Nothing could be clearer to all concerned
than that i am not a policeman.

Meanwhile the tea regressed.

Kipling again H. G. Wells, and Anatole France shook hands again and yet again
shook again hands again, the former coachman with a pipewrench of the again latter then opening a box of newly without exaggeration shot with some difficulty sardines. Mr. Wiggin took Wrs. Miggin's harm in is, extinguishing the spittoon by a candle furnished by courtesy of the management on Thursdays, opposite which a
church stood perfectly upright but not piano item: a watermelon causes indigestion
to William Cullen Longfellow's small negro son, Henry Wadsworth Bryant.

By this time, however, the flight of crows had ceased. I withdrew my hands from
the tennis racket. All was over. One brief convulsive octopus, and then our hero
folded his umbrella.

It seemed too beautiful.

Let us perhaps excuse me if i repeat himself : these, or nearly these, were the not
unpainful thoughts which occupied the subject of our attention; to speak even less

objectively, i was horribly scared i would actually fall off the rail before the
really train after all arrived. If i should have made this perfectly clear, it
entirely would have been not my fault.

42

the moon looked into my window

the moon looked into my window
it touched me with its small hands
and with curling infantile
fingers it understood my eyes cheeks mouth
its hands(slipping)felt of my necktie wandered
against my shirt and into my body the
sharp things fingered tinily my heart life

the little hands withdrew, jerkily, themselves

quietly they began playing with a button
the moon smiled she
let go my vest and crept
through the window
she did not fall
she went creeping along the air

over houses

roofs

And out of the east toward
her a fragile light bent gatheringly

43

touching you i say

touching you i say(it being Spring
and night)"let us go a very little beyond
the last road—there's something to be found"

and smiling you answer "every thing
turns into something else, and slips away....
(these leaves are Thingish with moondrool
and i'm ever so very little afraid")

I say

"along this particular road the moon if you'll
notice follows us like a big yellow dog. You

don't believe? look back.(Along the sand
behind us, a big yellow dog that's....now it's red
a big red dog that may be owned by who
knows)

only turn a little your. so. And

there's the moon, there is something faithful and mad"

43

touching you i say

touching you i say(it being Spring
and night)"let us go a very little beyond
the last road—there's something to be found"

and smiling you answer "every thing
turns into something else, and slips away....
(these leaves are Thingish with moondrool
and i'm ever so very little afraid")

I say

"along this particular road the moon if you'll
notice follows us like a big yellow dog. You

don't believe? look back.(Along the sand
behind us, a big yellow dog that's....now it's red
a big red dog that may be owned by who
knows)

only turn a little your. so. And

there's the moon, there is something faithful and mad"

42

the moon looked into my window

the moon looked into my window
it touched me with its small hands
and with curling infantile
fingers it understood my eyes cheeks mouth
its hands(slipping)felt of my necktie wandered
against my shirt and into my body the
sharp things fingered tinily my heart life

the little hands withdrew, jerkily, themselves

quietly they began playing with a button
the moon smiled she
let go my vest and crept
through the window
she did not fall
she went creeping along the air

over houses

roofs

And out of the east toward
her a fragile light bent gatheringly

44

if there are any heavens

if there are any heavens my mother will(all by herself)have
one. It will not be a pansy heaven nor
a fragile heaven of lilies-of-the-valley but
it will be a heaven of blackred roses

my father will be(deep like a rose
tall like a rose)

standing near my

swaying over her
(silent)
with eyes which are really petals and see

nothing with the face of a poet really which
is a flower and not a face with
hands
which whisper
This is my beloved my

(suddenly in sunlight
he will bow,
& the whole garden will bow)

45

Love Is A Place

Love is a place
& through this place of
love move
(with brightness of peace)
all places

yes is a world
& in this world of
yes live
(skilfully curled)
all worlds

46

Nothing False And Possible Is Love

Nothing false and possible is love
(who's imagined, therefore is limitless)
love's to giving as to keeping's give;
as yes is to if, love is to yes

must's a schoolroom in the month of may:
life's the deathboard where all now turns when
(love's a universe beyond obey
or command, reality or un-)

proudly depths above why's first because
(faith's last doubt and humbly heights below)
kneeling, we-true lovers-pray that us
will ourselves continue to outgrow

all whose mosts if you have known and i've
only we our least begin to guess.

47

Speaking Of Love

speaking of love(of
which Who knows the
meaning; or how dreaming
becomes

if your heart's mind)i
guess a grassblade
Thinks beyond or
around(as poems are

made)Our picking it. this
caress that laugh
both quickly signify
life's only half(through

deep weather then
or none let's feel
all) mind in mind flesh
In flesh succeeding disappear

48

I Am A Beggar Always

i am a beggar always
who begs in your mind

(slightly smiling, patient, unspeaking
with a sign on his
chest
BLIND)yes i

am this person of whom somehow
you are never wholly rid(and who

does not ask for more than
just enough dreams to
live on)
         after all, kid

you might as well
toss him a few thoughts

a little love preferably,
anything which you can't
pass off on other people: for

instance a
plugged promise-

the he will maybe (hearing something
fall into his hat)go wandering
after it with fingers; till having

found
what was thrown away
                         himself
taptaptaps out of your brain, hopes, life
to(carefully turning a
corner)never bother you any more

instance a
plugged promise-

the he will maybe (hearing something
fall into his hat)go wandering
after it with fingers; till having

found
what was thrown away
                      himself
taptaptaps out of your brain, hopes, life
to(carefully turning a
corner)never bother you any more

48

I Am A Beggar Always

i am a beggar always
who begs in your mind

(slightly smiling, patient, unspeaking
with a sign on his
chest
BLIND)yes i

am this person of whom somehow
you are never wholly rid(and who

does not ask for more than
just enough dreams to
live on)
          after all, kid

you might as well
toss him a few thoughts

a little love preferably,
anything which you can't
pass off on other people: for

49

You Being In Love

you being in love
will tell who softly asks in love,

am i separated from your body smile brain hands merely
to become the jumping puppets of a dream? oh i mean:
entirely having in my careful how
careful arms created this at length
inexcusable, this inexplicable pleasure-you go from several
persons: believe me that strangers arrive
when i have kissed you into a memory
slowly, oh seriously
-that since and if you disappear

solemnly
myselves
ask "life, the question how do i drink dream smile

and how do i prefer this face to another and
why do i weep eat sleep-what does the whole intend"
they wonder. oh and they cry "to be, being, that i am alive
this absurd fraction in its lowest terms
with everything cancelled

but shadows
-what does it all come down to? love? Love
if you like and i like, for the reason that i
hate people and lean out of this window is love, love
and the reason that i laugh and breathe is oh love and the reason
that i do not fall into this street is love."

50

you said Is

you said Is
there anything which
is dead or alive more beautiful
than my body, to have in your fingers
(trembling ever so little)?
      Looking into
your eyes Nothing, i said, except the
air of spring smelling of never and forever.

….and through the lattice which moved as
if a hand is touched by a
hand(which
moved as though
fingers touch a girl's
breast,
lightly)
    Do you believe in always, the wind
said to the rain
I am too busy with
my flowers to believe, the rain answered

51

the mind is its own beautiful prisoner

the mind is its own beautiful prisoner.
Mine looked long at the sticky moon
opening in dusk her new wings

then decently hanged himself, one afternoon.

The last thing he saw was you
naked amid unnaked things,

your flesh, a succinct wandlike animal,
a little strolling with the futile purr
of blood; your sex squeaked like a billiard-cue
chalking itself, as not to make an error,
with twists spontaneously methodical.
He suddenly tasted worms windows and roses

he laughed, and closed his eyes as a girl closes
her left hand upon a mirror.

52

Your Little Voice…

your little voice
Over the wires came leaping
and i felt suddenly
dizzy
With the jostling and shouting of merry flowers
wee skipping high-heeled flames
courtesied before my eyes
or twinkling over to my side
Looked up
with impertinently exquisite faces
floating hands were laid upon me
I was whirled and tossed into delicious dancing
up
Up
with the pale important
stars and the Humorous
moon
dear girl
How i was crazy how i cried when i heard
over time
and tide and death
leaping
Sweetly
your voice

53

this is the garden: colours come and go

this is the garden: colours come and go,
frail azures fluttering from night's outer wing
strong silent greens serenely lingering,
absolute lights like baths of golden snow.
This is the garden pursed lips do blow
upon cool flutes within wide glooms, and sing
(of harps celestial to the quivering string)
invisible faces hauntingly and slow.

This is the garden. Time shall surely reap
and on Death's blade lie many a flower curled,
in other lands where other songs be sung;
yet stand They here enraptured, as among
The slow deep trees perpetual of sleep
some silver-fingered fountain steals the world.

53

this is the garden: colours come and go

this is the garden: colours come and go,
frail azures fluttering from night's outer wing
strong silent greens serenely lingering,
absolute lights like baths of golden snow.
This is the garden pursed lips do blow
upon cool flutes within wide glooms, and sing
(of harps celestial to the quivering string)
invisible faces hauntingly and slow.

This is the garden.   Time shall surely reap
and on Death's blade lie many a flower curled,
in other lands where other songs be sung;
yet stand They here enraptured, as among
The slow deep trees perpetual of sleep
some silver-fingered fountain steals the world.

52

Your Little Voice…

your little voice
Over the wires came leaping
and i felt suddenly
dizzy
With the jostling and shouting of merry flowers
wee skipping high-heeled flames
courtesied before my eyes
or twinkling over to my side
Looked up
with impertinently exquisite faces
floating hands were laid upon me
I was whirled and tossed into delicious dancing
up
Up
with the pale important
stars and the Humorous
moon
dear girl
How i was crazy how i cried when i heard
over time
and tide and death
leaping
Sweetly
your voice

54

Sometimes I Am Alive Because With

sometimes i am alive because with
me her alert treelike body sleeps
which i will feel slowly sharpening
becoming distinct with love slowly,
who in my shoulder sinks sweetly teeth
until we shall attain the Spring smelling
intense large together coloured instant

the moment pleasantly frightful

when, her mouth suddenly rising, wholly
begins with mine fiercely to fool
(and from my thighs which shrug and pant
a murdering rain leapingly reaches the upward singular
deepest flower which she
carries in a gesture of her hips)

55

My Love

my love
thy hair is one kingdom
the king whereof is darkness
thy forehead is a flight of flowers
thy head is a quick forest
filled with sleeping birds
thy breasts are swarms of white bees
upon the bough of thy body
thy body to me is April
in those armpits is the approach of spring
thy thighs are white horses yoked to a chariot
of kings
they are the striking of a good minstrel
between them is always a pleasant song
my love
thy head is a casket
of the cool jewel of thy mind
the hair of thy head is one warrior
innocent of defeat
thy hair upon thy shoulders is an army
with victory and with trumpets
thy legs are the trees of dreaming

whose fruit is the very eatage of forgetfulness
thy lips are satraps in scarlet
in whose kiss is the combinings of kings
thy wrists
are holy
which are the keepers of the keys of thy blood
thy feet upon thy ankles are flowers in vases
of silver
in thy beauty is the dilemma of flutes
thy eyes are the betrayal
of bells comprehended through incense.

56

i have loved, let us see if that's all

i have loved, let us see if that's all.
Bit into you as teeth, in the stone
of a musical fruit. My lips pleasantly groan
on your taste. Jumped the quick wall

of your smile into stupid gardens
if this were not enough (not really enough
pulled one before one the vague tough

exquisite flowers, whom hardens
richly, darkness. On the whole
possibly have i loved….you)
sheath before sheath

stripped to the Odour. (and here's what WhoEver will
know
Had you as bite teeth;
i stood with you as a foal

stands but as the trees, lay, which grow

57

Raise The Shade

raise the shade
will youse dearie?
rain
wouldn't that

get yer goat but
we don't care do
we dearie we should
worry about the rain

huh
dearie?
yknow
i'm

sorry for awl the
poor girls that
gets up god
knows when every

day of their
lives
aint you,
        oo-oo.   dearie

not so
hard dear

you're killing me

58

will suddenly trees leap from winter and will

will suddenly trees leap from winter and will

the stabbing music of your white youth
wounded by my arms' bothness
(say a twilight lifting the fragile skill
of new leaves' voices, and sharp lips of spring
simply joining with the wonderless
city's sublime cheap distinct mouth)

do the exact human comely thing?

(or will the fleshless moments go and go

across this dirtied pane where softly preys
the grey and perpendicular Always-
or possibly there drift a pulseless blur
of paleness;
the unswift mouths of snow
insignificantly whisper…

59

It May Not Always Be So

it may not always be so; and i say
that if your lips, which i have loved, should touch
another's, and your dear strong fingers clutch
his heart, as mine in time not far away;
if on another's face your sweet hair lay
in such a silence as i know, or such
great writhing words as, uttering overmuch,
stand helplessly before the spirit at bay;
if this should be, i say if this should be—
you of my heart, send me a little word;
that i may go unto him, and take his hands,
saying, Accept all happiness from me.
Then shall i turn my face, and hear one bird
sing terribly afar in the lost lands.

60

May My Heart Always Be Open To Little

may my heart always be open to little
birds who are the secrets of living
whatever they sing is better than to know
and if men should not hear them men are old

may my mind stroll about hungry
and fearless and thirsty and supple
and even if it's sunday may i be wrong
for whenever men are right they are not young

and may myself do nothing usefully
and love yourself so more than truly
there's never been quite such a fool who could fail
pulling all the sky over him with one smile

61

because i love you

because i love you)last night

clothed in sealace
appeared to me
your mind drifting
with chuckling rubbish
of pearl weed coral and stones;

lifted,and(before my
eyes sinking)inward, fled;softly
your face smile breasts gargled
by death rowned only

again carefully through deepness to rise
these your wrists
thighs feet hands

poising
     to again utterly disappear;
rushing gently swiftly creeping
through my dreams last
night,all of your
body with its spirit floated
(clothed only in

the tide's acute weaving murmur

62

if i love You

if i love You
(thickness means
worlds inhabited by roamingly
stern bright faeries

if you love
me) distance is mind carefully
luminous with innumerable gnomes
Of complete dream

if we love each (shyly)
other, what clouds do or Silently
Flowers resembles beauty
less than our breathing

63

In Time Of Daffodils

In time of daffodils (who know the goal of living is to grow)
forgetting why, remember how
in time of lilacs who proclaim
the aim of waking is to dream,
remember so(forgetting seem)
in time of roses(who amaze
our now and here with paradise)
forgetting if, remember yes
in time of all sweet things beyond
whatever mind may comprehend,
remember seek(forgetting find)
and in a mystery to be
(when time from time shall set us free)
forgetting me, remember me

64

In The Rain

In the rain-
darkness, the sunset
being sheathed i sit and
think of you
the holy
city which is your face
your little cheeks the streets
of smiles
your eyes half-
thrush
half-angel and your drowsy
lips where float flowers of kiss

and
there is the sweet shy pirouette
your hair
and then
your dance song
soul.rarely-beloved
a single star is
uttered, and i
think of you

65

It Is At Moments After I Have Dreamed

It is at moments after i have dreamed
of the rare entertainment of your eyes,
when(being fool to fancy)i have deemed
with your peculiar mouth my heart made wise;
at moments when the glassy darkness holds

the genuine apparition of your smile
(it was through tears always)and silence moulds
such strangeness as was mine a little while;

moments when my once more illustrious arms
are filled with fascination, when my breast
wears the intolerant brightness of your charms:

one pierced moment whiter than the rest

– turning from the tremendous lie of sleep
i watch the roses of the day grow deep.

66

Nothing False And Possible Is Love

nothing false and possible is love
(who's imagined, therefore is limitless)
love's to giving as to keeping's give;
as yes is to if, love is to yes

must's a schoolroom in the month of may:
life's the deathboard where all now turns when
(love's a universe beyond obey
or command, reality or un-)

proudly depths above why's first because
(faith's last doubt and humbly heights below)
kneeling, we-true lovers-pray that us
will ourselves continue to outgrow

all whose mosts if you have known and i've
only we our least begin to guess

67

i thank You God for most this amazing

i thank You God for most this amazing
day: for the leaping greenly spirits of trees
and a blue true dream of sky; and for everything
which is natural which is infinite which is yes
(i who have died am alive again today,
and this is the sun's birthday; this is the birth
day of life and of love and wings: and of the gay
great happening illimitably earth)
how should tasting touching hearing seeing
breathing any—lifted from the no
of all nothing—human merely being
doubt unimaginable You?
(now the ears of my ears awake and
now the eyes of my eyes are opened)

68

Picasso

Picasso
you give us things
which
bulge:grunting lungs pumped full of sharp thick mind

you make us shrill
presents always
shut in the sumptuous screech of
simplicity

(out of the
black unbunged
Something gushes vaguely a squeak of planes
or

between squeals of
Nothing grabbed with circular shrieking tightness
solid screams whispers.)
Lumberman of the Distinct

your brain's
axe only chops hugest inherent
Trees of Ego, from
whose living and biggest

bodies lopped
of every
prettiness

you hew form truly

69

if i should sleep with a lady called death

if i should sleep with a lady called death
get another man with firmer lips
to take your new mouth in his teeth
(hips pumping pleasure into hips)

Seeing how the limp huddling string
of your smile over his body squirms
kissingly, i will bring you every spring
handfuls of little normal worms.

Dress deftly your flesh in stupid stuffs,
phrase the immense weapon of your hair.
Understanding why his eye laughs,
i will bring you every year

something which is worth the whole,
an inch of nothing for your soul.

70

somewhere i have never travelled, gladly beyond

somewhere i have never travelled, gladly beyond
any experience, your eyes have their silence:
in your most frail gesture are things which enclose me,
or which i cannot touch because they are too near

your slightest look easily will unclose me
though i have closed myself as fingers,
you open always petal by petal myself as Spring opens
(touching skilfully, mysteriously)her first rose

or if your wish be to close me, i and
my life will shut very beautifully, suddenly,
as when the heart of this flower imagines
the snow carefully everywhere descending;

nothing which we are to perceive in this world equals
the power of your intense fragility: whose texture
compels me with the colour of its countries,
rendering death and forever with each breathing

(i do not know what it is about you that closes
and opens; only something in me understands
the voice of your eyes is deeper than all roses)
nobody, not even the rain, has such small hands

71

My sweet old etcetera

my sweet old etcetera
aunt lucy during the recent

war could and what
is more did tell you just
what everybody was fighting

for,
my sister

Isabel created hundreds
(and
hundreds)of socks not to
mention fleaproof earwarmers
etcetera wristers etcetera, my
mother hoped that

I would die etcetera
bravely of course my father used
to become hoarse talking about how it was
a privilege and if only he
could meanwhile my

self etcetera lay quietly
in the deep mud et
cetera
(dreaming,
et
cetera, of
Your smile
eyes knees and of your Etcetera

72

here's to opening and upward, to leaf and to sap

here's to opening and upward, to leaf and to sap
and to your(in my arms flowering so new)
self whose eyes smell of the sound of rain

and here's to silent certainly mountains; and to
a disappearing poet of always, snow
and to morning; and to morning's beautiful friend
twilight(and a first dream called ocean)and

let must or if be damned with whomever's afraid
down with ought with because with every brain
which thinks it thinks, nor dares to feel(but up
with joy; and up with laughing and drunkenness)

here's to one undiscoverable guess
of whose mad skill each world of blood is made
(whose fatal songs are moving in the moon

73

It is funny, you will be gone some day

It is funny, you will be gone some day.
By you the mouth hair eyes, and i mean
the unique and nervously obscene

need;it's funny. They will all be gone

knead of lustfulhunched deeplytoplay
lips and stare the gross fuzzy-pash
-gone-and the dark gold delicately smash....
grass, and the stars, of my shoulder in stead.

It is a funny, thing. And you will be

and i and all the days and nights that matter
knocked by sun moon jabbed jerked with ecstasy
....tremble (not knowing how much better

than me will you like the rain's face and

the rich improbable hands of the Wind)

74

O sweet spontaneous

O sweet spontaneous
earth how often have
the
doting

   fingers of
prurient philosophers pinched
and
poked

thee
, has the naughty thumb
of science prodded
thy

   beauh , how
often have religions taken
thee upon their scraggy knees
squeezing and

buffeting thee that thou mightest conceive
gods
    (but
true

to the incomparable
couch of death thy
rhythmic
lover

   thou answerest

them only with

      spring)

buffeting thee that thou mightest conceive
gods
   (but
true

to the incomparable
couch of death thy
rhythmic
lover

   thou answerest

them only with

      spring)

74

O sweet spontaneous

O sweet spontaneous
earth how often have
the
doting

   fingers of
prurient philosophers pinched
and
poked

thee
, has the naughty thumb
of science prodded
thy

   beauty , how
often have religions taken
thee upon their scraggy knees
squeezing and

75

may my heart always be open to little

may my heart always be open to little
birds who are the secrets of living
whatever they sing is better than to know
and if men should not hear them men are old

may my mind stroll about hungry
 and fearless and thirsty and supple
and even if it's sunday may i be wrong
        for whenever men are right they are not young

and may myself do nothing usefully
and love yourself so more than truly
there's never been quite such a fool who could fail
pulling all the sky over him with one smile

76

old age sticks

old age sticks
up Keep
Off
signs)&

youth yanks them
down(old
age
cries No

Tres)&(pas)
youth laughs
(sing
old age

scolds Forbid
den Stop
Must
n't Don't

&)youth goes
right on
gr
owing old

77

little tree

LITTLE tree
little silent Christmas tree
you are so little
you are more like a flower
who found you in the green forest
and were you very sorry to come away?
see i will comfort you
because you smell so sweetly
i will kiss your cool bark
and hug you safe and tight
just as your mother would,
only don't be afraid
look the spangles
that sleep all the year in a dark box
dreaming of being taken out and allowed to shine,
the balls the chains red and gold the fluffy threads,
put up your little arms
and i'll give them all to you to hold
every finger shall have its ring
and there won't be a single place dark or unhappy
then when you're quite dressed
you'll stand in the window for everyone to see

and how they'll stare!
oh but you'll be very proud
and my little sister and i will take hands
and looking up at our beautiful tree
we'll dance and sing
"Noel Noel"

78

I Have Found What You Are Like

i have found what you are like
the rain,

    (Who feathers frightened fields
with the superior dust-of-sleep. wields

easily the pale club of the wind
and swirled justly souls of flower strike

the air in utterable coolness

deeds of green thrilling light
              with thinned

new fragile yellows
        lurch and. press

—in the woods
        which
            stutter
                and
                    sing
And the coolness of your smile is
stirring of birds between my arms; but
i should rather than anything
have(almost when hugeness will shut
quietly)almost,
       your kiss

79

my father moved through dooms of love

my father moved through dooms of love
through sames of am through haves of give,
singing each morning out of each night
my father moved through depths of height

this motionless forgetful where
turned at his glance to shining here;
that if (so timid air is firm)
under his eyes would stir and squirm

newly as from unburied which
floats the first who, his april touch
drove sleeping selves to swarm their fates
woke dreamers to their ghostly roots

and should some why completely weep
my father's fingers brought her sleep:
vainly no smallest voice might cry
for he could feel the mountains grow.

Lifting the valleys of the sea
my father moved through griefs of joy;
praising a forehead called the moon
singing desire into begin

79

my father moved through dooms of love

my father moved through dooms of love
through sames of am through haves of give,
singing each morning out of each night
my father moved through depths of height

this motionless forgetful where
turned at his glance to shining here;
that if (so timid air is firm)
under his eyes would stir and squirm

newly as from unburied which
floats the first who, his april touch
drove sleeping selves to swarm their fates
woke dreamers to their ghostly roots

and should some why completely weep
my father's fingers brought her sleep:
vainly no smallest voice might cry
for he could feel the mountains grow.

Lifting the valleys of the sea
my father moved through griefs of joy;
praising a forehead called the moon
singing desire into begin

78

I Have Found What You Are Like

i have found what you are like
the rain,

    (Who feathers frightened fields
with the superior dust-of-sleep. wields

easily the pale club of the wind
and swirled justly souls of flower strike

the air in utterable coolness

deeds of green thrilling light
              with thinned

new fragile yellows
        lurch and. press

—in the woods
        which
            stutter
                and
                    sing
And the coolness of your smile is
stirring of birds between my arms; but
i should rather than anything
have(almost when hugeness will shut
quietly)almost,
        your kiss

joy was his song and joy so pure
a heart of star by him could steer
and pure so now and now so yes
the wrists of twilight would rejoice

keen as midsummer's keen beyond
conceiving mind of sun will stand,
so strictly (over utmost him
so hugely) stood my father's dream

his flesh was flesh his blood was blood:
no hungry man but wished him food;
no cripple wouldn't creep one mile
uphill to only see him smile.

Scorning the Pomp of must and shall
my father moved through dooms of feel;
his anger was as right as rain
his pity was as green as grain

septembering arms of year extend
less humbly wealth to foe and friend
than he to foolish and to wise
offered immeasurable is

proudly and (by octobering flame
beckoned) as earth will downward climb,
so naked for immortal work
his shoulders marched against the dark

his sorrow was as true as bread:
no liar looked him in the head;

if every friend became his foe
he'd laugh and build a world with snow.

My father moved through theys of we,
singing each new leaf out of each tree
(and every child was sure that spring
danced when she heard my father sing)

then let men kill which cannot share,
let blood and flesh be mud and mire,
scheming imagine, passion willed,
freedom a drug that's bought and sold

giving to steal and cruel kind,
a heart to fear, to doubt a mind,
to differ a disease of same,
conform the pinnacle of am

though dull were all we taste as bright,
bitter all utterly things sweet,
maggoty minus and dumb death
all we inherit, all bequeath

and nothing quite so least as truth
—i say though hate were why men breathe—
because my Father lived his soul
love is the whole and more than all

80

i am a little church

i am a little church(no great cathedral) –
i do not worry if briefer days grow briefest,
i am not sorry when sun and rain make april

my life is the life of the reaper and the sower;
my prayers are prayers of earth's own clumsily striving
(finding and losing and laughing and crying)children
whose any sadness or joy is my grief or my gladness

around me surges a miracle of unceasing
birth and glory and death and resurrection:
over my sleeping self float flaming symbols
of hope, and i wake to a perfect patience of mountains

i am a little church(far from the frantic
world with its rapture and anguish)at peace with nature –
i do not worry if longer nights grow longest;
i am not sorry when silence becomes singing

winter by spring, i lift my diminutive spire to
merciful Him Whose only now is forever:
standing erect in the deathless truth of His presence
(welcoming humbly His light and proudly His darkness)

81

as freedom is a breakfastfood

as freedom is a breakfastfood
or truth can live with right and wrong
or molehills are from mountains made
—long enough and just so long
will being pay the rent of seem
and genius please the talentgang
and water most encourage flame

as hatracks into peachtrees grow
or hopes dance best on bald men's hair
and every finger is a toe
and any courage is a fear
—long enough and just so long
will the impure think all things pure
and hornets wail by children stung

or as the seeing are the blind
and robins never welcome spring
nor flatfolk prove their world is round
nor dingsters die at break of dong
and common's rare and millstones float
—long enough and just so long
tomorrow will not be too late

worms are the words but joy's the voice
down shall go which and up come who
breasts will be breasts thighs will be thighs
deeds cannot dream what dreams can do
—time is a tree(this life one leaf)
but love is the sky and i am for you
just so long and long enough

82

there are so many tictoc

there are so many tictoc
clocks everywhere telling people
what toctic time it is for
tictic instance five toc minutes toc
past six tic

Spring is not regulated and does
not get out of order nor do
its hands a little jerking move
over numbers slowly

                    we do not
wind it up it has no weights
springs wheels inside of
its slender self no indeed dear
nothing of the kind.

(So, when kiss Spring comes
we'll kiss each kiss other on kiss the kiss
lips because tic clocks toc don't make
a toctic difference
to kiss kiss you and to
kiss me)

83

if in beginning twilight of winter

if in beginning twilight of winter will stand
(over a snowstopped silent world)one
spirit serenely truly himself;
and
alone only as greatness is alone—
one(above nevermoving all nowhere)
goldenly whole, prodigiously alive
most mercifully glorying keen star
whom she-and-he-like ifs of am perceive
(but believe scarcely may)certainly while
mute each inch of their murdered planet grows
more and enormously more less: until
her-and-his nonexistence vanishes
with also earth's
             --"dying" the ghost of you
whispers "is very pleasant" my ghost to

83

if in beginning twilight of winter

if in beginning twilight of winter will stand
(over a snowstopped silent world)one
spirit serenely truly himself;
and
alone only as greatness is alone—
one(above nevermoving all nowhere)
goldenly whole, prodigiously alive
most mercifully glorying keen star
whom she-and-he-like ifs of am perceive
(but believe scarcely may)certainly while
mute each inch of their murdered planet grows
more and enormously more less: until
her-and-his nonexistence vanishes
with also earth's
         --"dying" the ghost of you
whispers "is very pleasant" my ghost to

82

there are so many tictoc

there are so many tictoc
clocks everywhere telling people
what toctic time it is for
tictic instance five toc minutes toc
past six tic

Spring is not regulated and does
not get out of order nor do
its hands a little jerking move
over numbers slowly

                      we do not
wind it up it has no weights
springs wheels inside of
its slender self no indeed dear
nothing of the kind.

(So, when kiss Spring comes
we'll kiss each kiss other on kiss the kiss
lips because tic clocks toc don't make
a toctic difference
to kiss kiss you and to
kiss me)

84

thee will i praise between those rivers

(thee will i praise between those rivers whose
white voices pass upon forgetting(fail
me not)whose courseless waters are a gloat
of silver; o'er whose night three willows wail,
a slender dimness in the unshapeful hour
making dear moan in tones of stroked flower;
let not thy lust one threaded moment lose:
haste)the very shadowy sheep float
free upon terrific pastures pale,

whose tall mysterious shepherd lifts a cheek
tear troubled to the momentary wind
with guiding smile, lips wisely minced for blown
kisses, condemnatory fingers thinned
of pity—so he stands counting the moved
myriads wonderfully loved,
(hasten, it is the moment which shall seek
all blossoms that do learn, scents of not known
musics in whose careful eyes are dinned;

and the people of perfect darkness fills
his mind who will their hungering whispers hear
with weepings soundless, saying of "alas

we were chaste on earth we ghosts: hark to the sheer
cadence of our grey flesh in the gloom!
and still to be immortal is our doom;
but a rain frailly raging whom the hills
sink into and their sunsets, it shall pass.
Our feet tread sleepless meadows sweet with fear")

then be with me: unseriously seem
by the perusing greenness of thy thought
my golden soul fabulously to glue
in a superior terror; be thy taut
flesh silver, like the currency of faint
cities eternal—ere the sinless taint
of thy long sinful arms about me dream
shall my love wholly taste thee as a new
wine from steep hills by darkness softly brought—

(be with me in the sacred witchery
of almostness which May makes follow soon
on the sweet heels of passed afterday,
clothe thy soul's coming merely, with a croon
of mingling robes musically revealed
in rareness: let thy twain eyes deeply wield
a noise of petals falling silently
through the far-spaced possible nearaway
from huge trees drenched by a rounding moon)

85

When You Went Away It Was Morning

when you went away it was morning
(that is, big horses; light feeling up
streets; heels taking derbies (where?) a pup
hurriedly hunched over swill; one butting

trolley imposingly empty; snickering
shop doors unlocked by white-grub
faces) clothes in delicate hubbub

as you stood thinking of anything,

maybe the world....But i have wondered since
isn't it odd of you really to lie
a sharp agreeable flower between my

amused legs
          kissing with little dints

of april, making the obscene shy
******* tickle, laughing when i wilt and wince

86

Let it go

let it go – the
smashed word broken
open vow or
the oath cracked length
wise – let it go it
was sworn to
go

let them go – the
truthful liars and
the false fair friends
and the boths and
neithers – you must let them go they
were born
to go

let all go – the
big small middling
tall bigger really
the biggest and all
things – let all go
dear
so comes love

87

Spring is past, and Summer's past

Spring is past, and Summer's past,
  Autumn's come, and going;
Weather seems as though at last
  We might get some snowing.
Spring was good, and Summer better,
  But the best of all is waiting,-
Madame Winter-don't forget her.-
  O
      You
          Skating!

Spring we welcomed when we met,
  Summer was a blessing;
Autumn points to school, but yet
  Let's be acquiescing.
Spring had many precious pleasures;
  Winter's on a different rating;
She has greater, richer treasures,-
  O
      You
          Skating!

Gleam of ice, and glint of steel,
 Jolly, snappy weather;
Glide on ice and joy of zeal,
 All, alone, together.
Fickle Spring! Who can imprint her?-
 Faithless while she's captivating;
Here's to trusty Madame Winter.-
   O

      You
         Skating!

88

Maggie And Milly And Molly And May

maggie and milly and molly and may
went down to the beach(to play one day)

and maggie discovered a shell that sang
so sweetly she couldn't remember her troubles, and

milly befriended a stranded star
whose rays five languid fingers were;

and molly was chased by a horrible thing
which raced sideways while blowing bubbles: and

may came home with a smooth round stone
as small as a world and as large as alone.

For whatever we lose(like a you or a me)
it's always ourselves we find in the sea

89

dive for dreams

dive for dreams
or a slogan may topple you
(trees are their roots
and wind is wind)

trust your heart
if the seas catch fire
(and live by love
though the stars walk backward)

honour the past
but welcome the future
(and dance your death
away at this wedding)

never mind a world
with its villains or heroes
(for god likes girls
and tomorrow and the earth)

90

as we lie side by side

as
we lie side by side
my little breasts become two sharp delightful strutting
towers and
i shove hotly the lovingness of my belly against you
your arms are
young;
Your arms will convince me, in the complete silence
speaking
upon my body
their ultimate slender language.
do not laugh at my thighs.
there is between my big legs a crisp city.
when you touch me
it is Spring in the city;
the streets beautifully writhe,
it is for you;
do not frighten them,
all the houses terribly tighten
upon your coming;
and they are glad
as you fill the streets of my city with children.

my love you are a bright mountain which feels.
you are a keen mountain and an eager island whose
lively slopes are based always in the me which is
shrugging,which is
under you and around you and forever: i am the hugging
sea.
O mountain you cannot escape me
your roots are anchored in my silence; therefore O
mountain
skillfully murder my breasts, still and always
i will hug you solemnly into me.

91

she, straddling my lap

she, straddling my lap,
hinges(wherewith I tongue each eager pap)
and, reaching down, by merely fingertips
the hungry Visitor steers to love's lips
Whom(justly as she now begins to sit,
almost by almost giving her sweet weight)
O, how those hot thighs juicily embrace!
and (instant by deep instant) as her face
watches, scarcely alive, that magic Feast
greedily disappearing least by least— —-
through what a dizzily palpitating host
(sharp inch by inch) swoons sternly my huge Guest!
until(quite when our touching bellies dream)
unvisibly love's furthest screts rhyme.

92

A Wind Has Blown The Rain Away And Blown

a wind has blown the rain away and blown
the sky away and all the leaves away,
and the trees stand. I think i too have known
autumn too long

      (and what have you to say,
wind wind wind—did you love somebody
and have you the petal of somewhere in your heart
pinched from dumb summer?
              O crazy daddy
of death dance cruelly for us and start

the last leaf whirling in the final brain
of air!)Let us as we have seen see
doom's integration..........a wind has blown the rain

away and the leaves and the sky and the
trees stand:
      the trees stand. The trees,
suddenly wait against the moon's face.

92

A Wind Has Blown The Rain Away And Blown

a wind has blown the rain away and blown
the sky away and all the leaves away,
and the trees stand. I think i too have known
autumn too long

      (and what have you to say,
wind wind wind—did you love somebody
and have you the petal of somewhere in your heart
pinched from dumb summer?
              O crazy daddy
of death dance cruelly for us and start

the last leaf whirling in the final brain
of air!)Let us as we have seen see
doom's integration.........a wind has blown the rain

away and the leaves and the sky and the
trees stand:
      the trees stand. The trees,
suddenly wait against the moon's face.

91

she, straddling my lap

she, straddling my lap,
hinges(wherewith I tongue each eager pap)
and, reaching down, by merely fingertips
the hungry Visitor steers to love's lips
Whom(justly as she now begins to sit,
almost by almost giving her sweet weight)
O, how those hot thighs juicily embrace!
and (instant by deep instant) as her face
watches, scarcely alive, that magic Feast
greedily disappearing least by least——-
through what a dizzily palpitating host
(sharp inch by inch) swoons sternly my huge Guest!
until(quite when our touching bellies dream)
unvisibly love's furthest screts rhyme.

93

the great advantage of being alive

the great advantage of being alive
(instead of undying)is not so much
that mind no more can disprove than prove
what heart may feel and soul may touch
— the great (my darling)happens to be
that love are in we, that love are in we

and here is a secret they never will share for whom create
is less than have
or one times one than when times where —
that we are in love, that we are in love:
with us they've nothing times nothing to do
(for love are in we am in i are in you)

this world(as timorous itsters all
to call their cowardice quite agree)
shall never discover our touch and feel
–for love are in we are in love are in we;
for you are and i am and we are(above
and under all possible worlds)in love

a billion brains may coax undeath
from fancied fact and spaceful time—
no heart can leap, no soul can breathe
but by the sizeless truth of a dream
whose sleep is the sky and the earth and the sea.
For love are in you am in i are in we

94

she being Brand

she being Brand
-new;and you
know consequently a
little stiff i was
careful of her and(having

thoroughly oiled the universal
joint tested my gas felt of
her radiator made sure her springs were O.

K.)i went right to it flooded-the-carburetor cranked her

up,slipped the
clutch(and then somehow got into reverse she
kicked what
the hell)next
minute i was back in neutral tried and

again slo-wly;bare,ly nudg. ing(my

lev-er Right-
oh and her gears being in

A 1 shape passed
from low through
second-in-to-high like
greasedlightning)just as we turned the corner of Divinity

avenue i touched the accelerator and give

her the juice, good

(it
was the first ride and believe i we was
happy to see how nice she acted right up to
the last minute coming back down by the Public
Gardens i slammed on
the
internalexpanding
&
externalcontracting
brakes Bothatonce and

brought allofher tremB
-ling
to a:dead.

stand-;
Still)

95

I will wade out

I will wade out
till my thighs are steeped in burn-
ing flowers
I will take the sun in my mouth
and leap into the ripe air
Alive
with closed eyes
to dash against darkness
in the sleeping curves of my
body
Shall enter fingers of smooth mastery
with chasteness of sea-girls
Will I complete the mystery
of my flesh I will rise
After a thousand years
lipping
flowers
And set my teeth in the silver of the moon

96

My Love Is Building A Building

my love is building a building
around you, a frail slippery
house, a strong fragile house
(beginning at the singular beginning

of your smile)a skilful uncouth
prison, a precise clumsy
prison(building thatandthis into Thus,
Around the reckless magic of your mouth)

my love is building a magic, a discrete
tower of magic and(as i guess)

when Farmer Death(whom fairies hate)shall

crumble the mouth-flower fleet
He'll not my tower,
               laborious, casual

where the surrounded smile
               hangs

                      breathless

97

Yours Is The Music For No Instrument

yours is the music for no instrument
yours the preposterous colour unbeheld

—mine the unbought contemptuous intent
till this our felsh merely shall be excelled
by speaking flower
              (if I have made songs

it does not greatly matter to the sun,
nor will rain care
              cautiously who prolongs
unserious twilight)Shadows have begun

the hair's worm huge, ecstatic, rathe....

yours are the poems i do not write.

In this at least we have got a bulge on death,
silence,and the keenly musical light

of sudden nothing....la bocca mia "he
kissed wholly trembling"

                      or so thought the lady.

97

Yours Is The Music For No Instrument

yours is the music for no instrument
yours the preposterous colour unbeheld

—mine the unbought contemptuous intent
till this our felsh merely shall be excelled
by speaking flower
                (if I have made songs

it does not greatly matter to the sun,
nor will rain care
                cautiously who prolongs
unserious twilight)Shadows have begun

the hair's worm huge, ecstatic, rathe....

yours are the poems i do not write.

In this at least we have got a bulge on death,
silence,and the keenly musical light

of sudden nothing....la bocca mia "he
kissed wholly trembling"

                or so thought the lady.

96

My Love Is Building A Building

my love is building a building
around you, a frail slippery
house, a strong fragile house
(beginning at the singular beginning

of your smile)a skilful uncouth
prison, a precise clumsy
prison(building thatandthis into Thus,
Around the reckless magic of your mouth)

my love is building a magic, a discrete
tower of magic and(as i guess)

when Farmer Death(whom fairies hate)shall

crumble the mouth-flower fleet
He'll not my tower,
          laborious, casual

where the surrounded smile
          hangs

               breathless

98

Who's Most Afraid Of Death? Thou

who's most afraid of death? thou
                art of him
utterly afraid, i love of thee
(beloved)this

          and truly i would be
near when his scythe takes crisply the whim
of thy smoothness.   and mark the fainting
murdered petals. with caving stem.

But of all most would i be one of them

round the hurt heart which do so frailly cling....)
i who am but imperfect in my fear

Or with thy mind against my mind, to hear
nearing our hearts' irrevocable play —
through the mysterious high futile day

an enormous stride
            (and drawing thy mouth toward

my mouth, steer our lost bodies carefully downward.

99

Now that

now that, more nearest even than your fate
and mine(or any truth beyond perceive)
quivers this miracle of summer night
her trillion secrets touchably alive
-while and all mysteries which i or you
(blinded by merely things believable)
could only fancy we should nevr know
are unimaginably ours to feel-
how should some world(we marvel)doubt,for just
sweet terrifying the particular
moment it takes one very falling most
(there: did you see it?) star to disapppear
that hugest whole creation may be less
incalculable than a single Kiss

100

2 little whos

2 little whos
(he and she)
under are this
wonderful tree

smiling stand
(all realms of where
and when beyond)
now and here

(far from a grown
-up i&you-
ful world of known)
who and who

(2 little ams
and over them this
aflame with dreams
incredible is)

e.e. cummings
American poet

Born: October 14, 1894, Cambridge, Massachusetts
Died: September 3, 1962, North Conway, New Hampshire

Timeline:

- October 14th 1894: Edward Estlin Cummings was born to Edward Cummings and Rebecca Haswell Clarke in Cambridge, Massachusetts.
- 1911-1915: He attended Harvard University and his first poems are published in a collection, *Eight Harvard Poets*.
- 1917: Cummings joins the ambulance corps for the war. Later he is imprisoned and writes about this experience in *The Enormous Room*.
- 1923: Cummings' first collection of poetry, *Tulips* and *Chimneys* is published.
- 1924: Marries Elaine Thayer in March, and they divorce in December.
- 1925: Receives the Dial award for "distinguished service to American letters". Cummings' XLI Poems is published, proving to the world his unique writing style.
- 1926: His father is killed in a car crash. His mother is injured, but survives. This moves him to write about his life experiences - "my father moves through dooms of love".
- 1924-1927: Cummings is employed as essay writer and portrait artist for Vanity Fair.
- May 1st, 1929: Marries Anne Barton
- 1932: Separates from Anne Barton and marries Marion Morehouse who stays with him until his death 30 years later.
- 1928 - Cummings' first play, HIM, is published.
- 1955: Begins a seven year career of poetry readings.
- September 3rd, 1962: e.e. Cummings passed away of a stroke at the age of 67.